P9-DMB-372

To My Precious daughter

A Gaggle of Giggles

by Joseph Rosenbloom,
Matt Rissinger, and Phil Yates

STERLING

New York / London

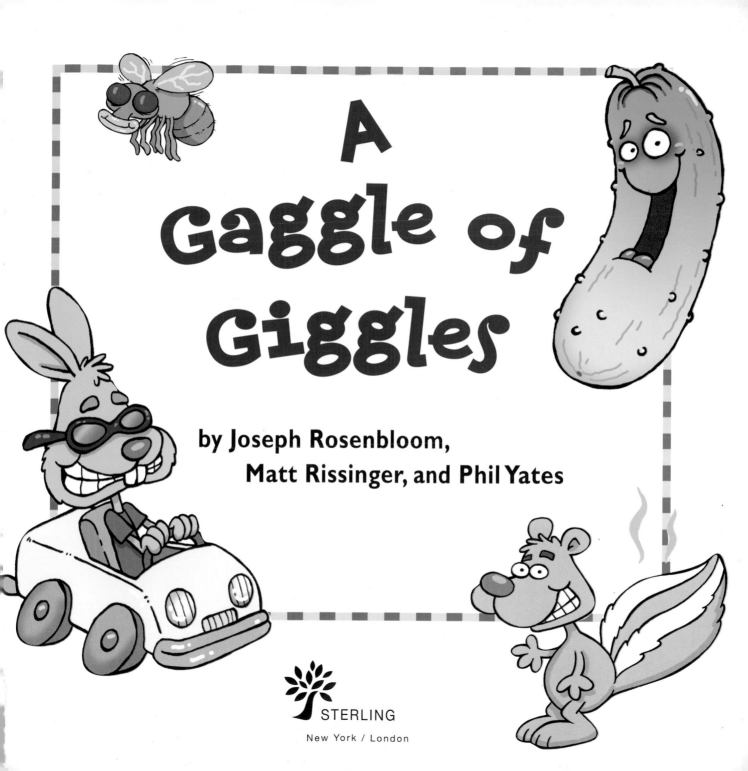

STERLING and the distinctive Sterling logo
are registered trademarks of Sterling Publishing Co., Inc.

Lot #:
10 9 8 7 6 5 4 3 2 1
07/10

This book is a compilation of 4 books originally published by Sterling Publishing Co., Inc.:
Giggle Fit®: Tricky Tongue-Twisters, text ©2001 by Joseph Rosenbloom
Giggle Fit®: Nutty Jokes, text ©2001 by Matt Rissinger and Phil Yates
Giggle Fit®: Silly Knock-Knocks, text ©2001 by Joseph Rosenbloom
Giggle Fit®: Goofy Riddles, text ©2001 by Joseph Rosenbloom

Published by Sterling Publishing Co., Inc.
387 Park Avenue South, New York, NY 10016
Distributed in Canada by Sterling Publishing
c/o Canadian Manda Group, 165 Dufferin Street
Toronto, Ontario, Canada M6K 3H6
Distributed in the United Kingdom by GMC Distribution Services
Castle Place, 166 High Street, Lewes, East Sussex, England BN7 1XU
Distributed in Australia by Capricorn Link (Australia) Pty. Ltd.
P.O. Box 704, Windsor, NSW 2756, Australia

Printed in China
All rights reserved

Sterling ISBN 978-1-4027-7768-4

For information about custom editions, special sales, premium and
corporate purchases, please contact Sterling Special Sales
Department at 800-805-5489 or specialsales@sterlingpublishing.com.

Chapter One

Tricky Tongue-Twisters

Bluebirds in blue birdbaths.
Bluebirds in blue birdbaths.
Bluebirds in blue birdbaths.

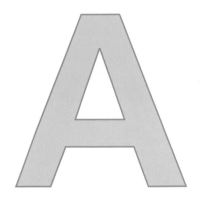

A

Aunt Edith's anteater.
Aunt Edith's anteater.
Aunt Edith's anteater.

Ava ate 80 eggs.
Ava ate 80 eggs.
Ava ate 80 eggs.

Ape cakes.
Ape cakes.
Ape cakes.

Build a big brick building.
Build a big brick building.
Build a big brick building.

Betty Botter bought a bit of butter.
"But," said she, "this butter's bitter.
If I put in in my batter, it will make my batter bitter.
But a bit of better butter — that would make my
        batter better."
So Betty Botter bought a bit of better butter
(Better than her bitter butter)
And made her bitter butter
A bit better.

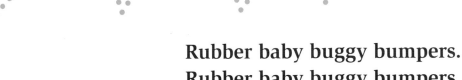

Rubber baby buggy bumpers.
Rubber baby buggy bumpers.
Rubber baby buggy bumpers.

C

Tricky crickets.
Tricky crickets.
Tricky crickets.

Cheap sausage stew.
Cheap sausage stew.
Cheap sausage stew.

Kooky cookies.
Kooky cookies.
Kooky cookies.

How many times can you say this in ten seconds?

Jerry chewed two chewy cherries.

Chris's craft crashed.
Chris's craft crashed.
Chris's craft crashed.

Cheap sheep soup.
Cheap sheep soup.
Cheap sheep soup.

Don't you dare dawdle, Darryl!
Don't you dare dawdle, Darryl!
Don't you dare dawdle, Darryl!

A dozen dim ding-dongs.
A dozen dim ding-dongs.
A dozen dim ding-dongs.

Ducks don't dunk doughnuts.
Ducks don't dunk doughnuts.
Ducks don't dunk doughnuts.

8

Eight eager eagles.
Eight eager eagles.
Eight eager eagles.

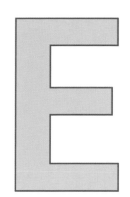

Edgar at 8 ate 8 eggs a day.
Edgar at 8 ate 8 eggs a day.
Edgar at 8 ate 8 eggs a day.

Elegant elephants.
Elegant elephants.
Elegant elephants.

Fried fresh fish.
Fried fresh fish.
Fried fresh fish.

Freckle-faced Freddy fidgets.
Freckle-faced Freddy fidgets.
Freckle-faced Freddy fidgets.

Five fat French fleas.
Five fat French fleas.
Five fat French fleas.

Greek grapes.
Greek grapes.
Greek grapes.

Good blood, bad blood.
Good blood, bad blood.
Good blood, bad blood.

Goats and ghosts.
Goats and ghosts.
Goats and ghosts.

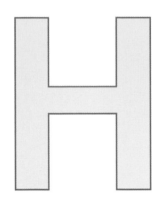

How many times can you say this in ten seconds?

Horse hairs are coarse hairs, of course.

Hiccup teacup.
Hiccup teacup.
Hiccup teacup.

Higgledy-Piggledy.
Higgledy-Piggledy.
Higgledy-Piggledy.

12

I see Isa's icy eyes.
I see Isa's icy eyes.
I see Isa's icy eyes.

Ike ships ice chips.
Ike ships ice chips.
Ike ships ice chips.

A gentle judge judges justly.
A gentle judge judges justly.
A gentle judge judges justly.

Jim jogs in the gym. Jane jogs in the jungle.

June sheep
sleep soundly.

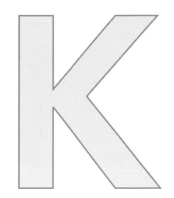

Come kick six sticks.
Come kick six sticks.
Come kick six sticks.

*How many times can you say this
in ten seconds?*
Kirk's starched shirts.

Kooky kite kits.
Kooky kite kits.
Kooky kite kits.

L

Luke likes licorice.
Luke likes licorice.
Luke likes licorice.

Lizzie's dizzy lizard.
Lizzie's dizzy lizard.
Lizzie's dizzy lizard.

How many times can you say this in ten seconds?
Loose loops.

Mummies munch much mush.
Mummies munch much mush.
Mummies munch much mush.

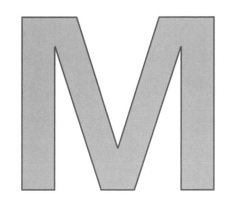

Moses supposes his toeses are roses,
But Moses supposes erroneously.
For nobody's toeses are posies of roses
As Moses supposes his toeses to be.

*How many times can you say
this in ten seconds?*
Michael's mouse
munched muffins.

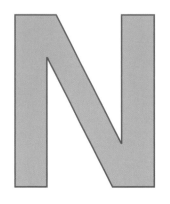

N

How many times can you say this in ten seconds?

No one knows Wayne.

There's no need to light a night light
On a light night like tonight,
For a night light's just a slight light,
On a light night like tonight.

Norse myths.
Norse myths.
Norse myths.

Nineteen nice knights.
Nineteen nice knights.
Nineteen nice knights.

Old oily corks.
Old oily corks.
Old oily corks.

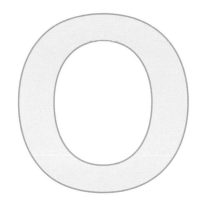

An oyster met an oyster,
And they were oysters two.
Two oysters met two oysters,
And they were oysters too.
Four oysters met a pint of milk,
And they were oyster stew.

Under the mother otter,
Uttered the other otter.

P

Picky pickpockets.
Picky pickpockets.
Picky pickpockets.

Preshrunk shirts.
Preshrunk shirts.
Preshrunk shirts.

Pooped purple pelicans.
Pooped purple pelicans.
Pooped purple pelicans.

20

Peter Piper picked a peck of
    pickled peppers,
A peck of pickled peppers,
Peter Piper picked.
If Peter Piper picked a peck of
    pickled peppers,
Where's the peck of pickled
    peppers Peter Piper
    picked?

Plain bun, plum bun.
Plain bun, plum bun.
Plain bun, plum bun.

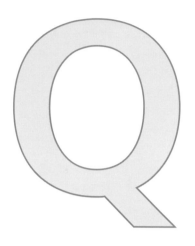

How many times can you say this in ten seconds?
Quick kiss.

Quincy! Quack quietly or quit quacking!
Quincy! Quack quietly or quit quacking!
Quincy! Quack quietly or quit quacking!

Really rich roaches wear wristwatches.

How many times can you say this in ten seconds?
A well-read redhead.

Raise Ruth's roof.
Raise Ruth's roof.
Raise Ruth's roof.

S

How many times can you say this in ten seconds?

Spicy fish sauce.

"Sure, the ship's ship-shape, sir!"

How many times can you say this in ten seconds?

Sloppy shortstops.

Sneak thieves seized the skis.
Sneak thieves seized the skis.
Sneak thieves seized the skis.

Stagecoach stops.
Stagecoach stops.
Stagecoach stops.

She sells seashells by the seashore.

T

A tree toad loved a she-toad
That lived up in a tree.
She was a three-toed tree toad,
But a two-toed toad was he.

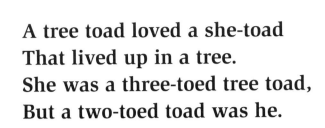

A tutor who tooted a flute
Tried to tutor two tooters to toot.
Said the two to the tutor,
"Is it harder to toot
Or to tutor two tooters to toot?"

*How many times can you say this
in ten seconds?*
Thistle thorns stick.

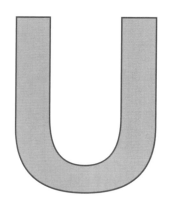

The U.S. twin-screw cruiser.
The U.S. twin-screw cruiser.
The U.S. twin-screw cruiser.

How many times can you say this in ten seconds?
Unique New York.

Uncle Upton's undies.
Uncle Upton's undies.
Uncle Upton's undies.

Vandals waxed Valerie's white van.
Vandals waxed Valerie's white van.
Vandals waxed Valerie's white van.

Valuable valley villas.
Valuable valley villas.
Valuable valley villas.

How many times can you say this in ten seconds?

Which veteran ventriloquist whistled?

Whether the weather be fine
Or whether the weather be not;
Whether the weather be cold,
Or whether the weather be hot;
We'll weather the weather
Whatever the weather,
Whether we like it or not.

*How many times can you say this
in ten seconds?*

An itchy rich witch.

Real wristwatch straps.

How much wood would a
    woodchuck chuck
If a woodchuck could chuck
    wood?
He would chuck the wood
    as much as he could
If a woodchuck could chuck
    wood.

White rings, round rings.
White rings, round rings.
White rings, round rings.

Wire-rimmed wheels.
Wire-rimmed wheels.
Wire-rimmed wheels.

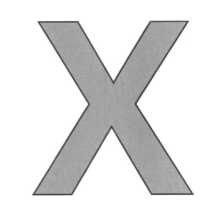

Ex-disk jockey.
Ex-disk jockey.
Ex-disk jockey.

Xmas wrecks perplex and vex.
Xmas wrecks perplex and vex.
Xmas wrecks perplex and vex.

Y

Yellow leather, red feather.

Yanking yellow yo-yos.
Yanking yellow yo-yos.
Yanking yellow yo-yos.

Local yokel jokes.

Z

This is a zither.
Is this a zither?

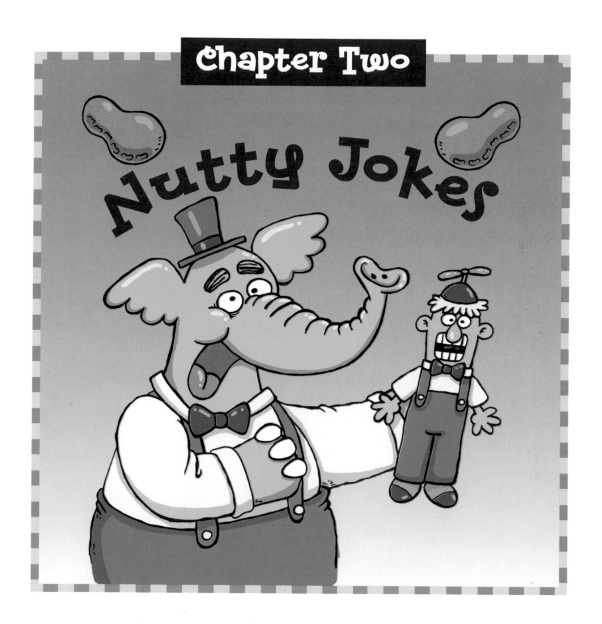

How can you tell the age of an elephant?
Count the candles on its birthday cake.

What's big and white and lives in the Sahara Desert?
A lost polar bear.

What's a polar bear's favorite vacation spot?
Brrrr-muda.

What cartoon animal weighs the least?
Skinny the Pooh.

What would you call a lion
that writes snappy songs?
King of the Jingle.

What would you get if you crossed a
baby kangaroo with a TV buff?
A pouch potato.

What would you get if you crossed a guppy with a
monkey?
A shrimpanzee.

What's brown and has 8 legs and a big trunk?
A spider coming home from a trip.

What kind of flowers would you give an absent-minded squirrel?
Forget-me-nuts.

What's an owl's favorite mystery?
A whooo-dunit.

What is a woodpecker's favorite kind of joke?
A knock-knock.

Where does a mother
octopus shop for clothes
for its children?
Squids 'R' Us.

What would you get if you crossed an
octopus and a cat?
An animal with 8 arms and 9 lives.

Why did the turtle see a psychiatrist?
He wanted to come out of his shell.

Why don't fish go on-line?
Because they're afraid of being caught in the Net.

What kinds of doctors make fish look beautiful?
Plastic sturgeons.

What's an eel's favorite card game?
Glow Fish.

What happened to the cat that swallowed a ball of wool?
It had mittens.

What do baby cats wear?
Diapurrrrs.

How do you know when your cat's been on the Internet?
Your mouse has teeth marks in it.

What did they name the dog
with the receding hairline?
Bald Spot.

What do you give a dog that
loves computers?
Doggie diskettes.

Why did the puppy go to the hair salon?
To get a shampoodle.

How do you turn a beagle into a bird?
Remove the B.

Why did the dog get a ticket?
For double barking.

What would you get if you crossed a dog with a chicken?
Pooched eggs.

In what age did the Sloppy-o-saurus live?
The Messy-zoic period.

What do dragons like
most about school?
The fire drills.

DRAGO the GREAT

Where do great dragons
end up?
In the Hall of Flame.

How do you give an elephant a bath?
First you find a very large rubber duckie.

How do you know when there's an elephant in your chocolate pudding?
When it's lumpier than usual.

What would you get if you crossed a parrot and an elephant?
An animal that tells you everything it remembers.

What do snakes do after a fight?
They hiss and make up.

What is a snake's
favorite subject?
SSScience.

What kind of snake wears dark glasses and a
trench coat?
A spy-thon.

What would you get if you crossed a snake with Bigfoot?

Ssss-quatch.

What would you call a snake that drinks too much coffee?

A hyper viper.

What would you get if you crossed an eight-foot snake with a five-foot snake?

Nothing. Snakes don't have feet.

What's a cat's favorite kind of computer?
A laptop.

Why did the computer squeak?
Because someone stepped on its mouse.

What kind of computer mail do mice exchange?
Eeek-mail.

Why did the computer go to the eye doctor?
To improve its website.

Why did the banana go to
the hospital?
It didn't peel so well.

What did cavemen eat
for lunch?
Club sandwiches.

Where do spies do their
shopping?
At the snooper market.

How do you make a cream puff?
Chase it around the block a few times.

What is a baker's favorite kind of book?
A who-donut.

What dessert can you eat in
the ocean?
Sponge cake.

Where do sheep buy their clothes?
Lamb shops.

What did the tie say to the hat?
"You go on ahead, I'll just hang around."

What animal goes "Baa-Baa-Woof"?
A sheepdog.

Where do cows stay when they go on a trip?
In moo-tels.

What do near-sighted ghosts wear?
Spook-tacles.

How do ghosts get to school?
On a ghoul bus.

What position did the ghost play on the soccer team?
Ghoulie.

Why didn't the skeleton go to the ball?

Because he had no body to go with.

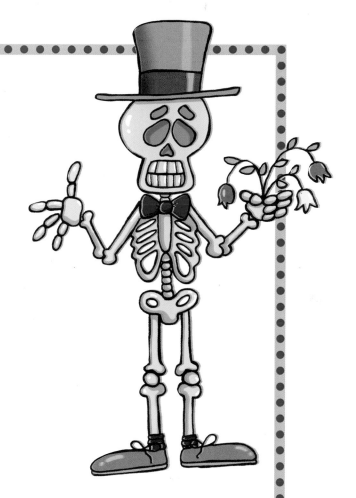

Why did the skeleton refuse to bungee jump?

He didn't have any guts.

What would you get if you crossed nursery rhymes with scary stories?

Mother Goosebumps.

What would you get if you crossed a vampire and a mummy?
Either a flying bandage or a gift-wrapped bat.

What do you call six vampires to go?
A Drac pack.

What would you get if you crossed a skunk with the Frankenstein monster?
Stinkenstein.

What did the chalkboard
say to the eraser?
   **"You rub me the
   wrong way."**

Why was the pony sent to the principal's
office?
   For horsing around.

Why was the chicken sent to the
principal's office?
   **Because it kept pecking on the
   other kids.**

Why did the squirrels get such low grades?
They drove the teacher nuts.

How did the flower do on the test?
It got all bees.

Why did the firefly do so well on the test?
It was very bright.

Why did King Kong wear a baseball glove to the airport?
He had to catch a plane.

Can kids learn to fly jet planes?
Yes, but they have to use training wheels.

What kind of clothes do parachutists wear?
Jumpsuits.

Why did the Christmas tree go to the hospital?
It had tinsel-itis.

What do trees watch on television?
Sap operas.

What grows on trees and is scared of wolves?
The three little figs.

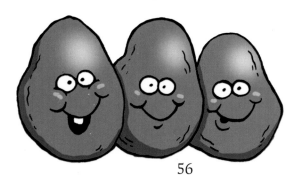

What do rabbits put on the backs of their cars?
Thumper stickers.

What kind of cars do rubber bands drive?
Stretch limos.

What happens when a frog is double-parked on a lily pad?
It's toad away.

What's yellow,
plastic, and holds
up banks?
A robber duckie.

Where do detectives sleep?
Under cover.

Why would Snow White make a great judge?
Because she is fairest of them all.

What would you get if you crossed a baseball player with a frog?
An outfielder who catches flies and then eats them.

Was the vampire race close?
Yes, it was neck and neck.

What kind of bee is always dropping the football?
A fumblebee.

What does a messy flea need?
A lousekeeper.

What should you do if you find Godzilla in your bed?
Sleep in the guest room.

What do witches like to do on the computer?

Use the spell checker.

What do you call a sorceress with a broken broom?

A witchhiker.

What do videos do on their days off?

They unwind.

What did one mule
say to the other mule?
**"I get a kick out
of you."**

What didn't King Arthur ever get
served at the Round Table?
A square meal.

Did you hear about the King
Arthur stamp?
It's for over-knight delivery.

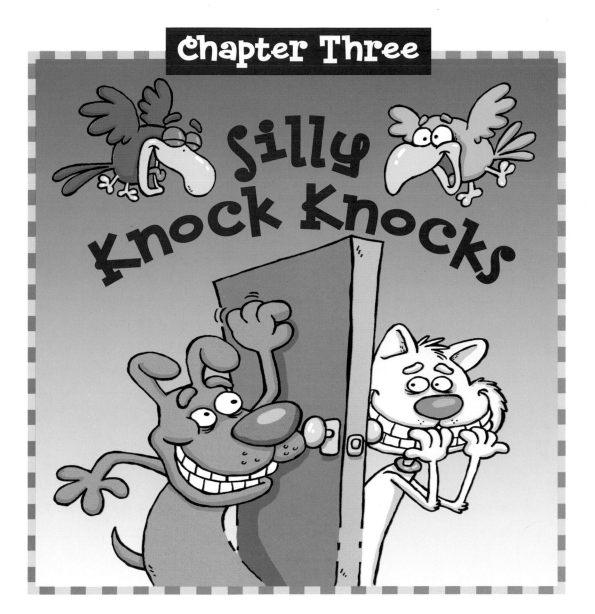

Knock-Knock. Who's there? Alaska.
Alaska who? Alaska my mother.

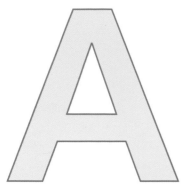

Knock-Knock.
  Who's there?
Anita.
  Anita who?
Anita rest.

Knock-Knock.
  Who's there?
Athena.
  Athena who?
Athena flying saucer.

Knock-Knock.
  Who's there?
Althea.
  Althea who?
Althea later, Alligator!

Knock-Knock.
Who's there?
Benny
Benny who?
Benny long time no see.

Knock-Knock.
Who's there?
Banana.

Knock-Knock.
Who's there?
Banana.

Knock-Knock.
Who's there?
Banana.

Knock-Knock.
Who's there?
Orange.
Orange who?
Orange you glad I didn't say Banana?

Knock-Knock.
Who's there?
Barbie.
Barbie who?
Barbie Q. Chicken.

Knock-Knock.
Who's there?
Beth.
Beth who?
Beth wishes, thweetie.

Knock-Knock.
Who's there?
Barbara.
Barbara who?
Barbara black sheep, have you any wool?

Knock-Knock.
  Who's there?
Canoe.
  Canoe who?
Canoe please get off my foot?

Knock-Knock.
  Who's there?
Cher.
  Cher who?
Cherlock Holmes.

Knock-Knock.
  Who's there?
Catch.
  Catch who?
Bless you!

Knock-Knock.
Who's there?
Dexter.
Dexter who?
Dexter halls with boughs of holly!

Knock-Knock.
Who's there?
Deluxe.
Deluxe who?
**Deluxe Ness
Monster.**

Knock-Knock.
Who's there?
Dora Belle.
Dora Belle who?
Dora Belle is broken so I knocked.

68

Knock-Knock.
Who's there?
Easter.
Easter who?
Easter anybody home?

Knock-Knock.
Who's there?
Eileen Dunn.
Eileen Dunn who?
Eileen Dunn the doorbell and it broke.

Knock-Knock.
Who's there?
Emmet.
Emmet who?
Emmet your service.

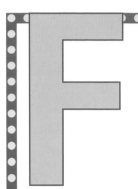

Knock-Knock.
    Who's there?
Flea.
    Flea who?
Flea blind mice.

Knock-Knock.
    Who's there?
Freddie.
    Freddie who?
**Freddie or not, here
I come.**

Knock-Knock.
    Who's there?
Fido.
    Fido who?
**Fido away, will you
miss me?**

Knock-Knock.
Who's there?
Gopher.
Gopher who?
Gopher the gold!

Knock-Knock.
Who's there?
Goat.
Goat who?
Goat to your room.

Knock-Knock.
Who's there?
Gorilla.
Gorilla who?
Gorilla cheese sandwich.

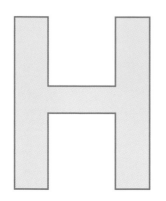

Knock-Knock.
  Who's there?
Harvey.
  Harvey who?
Harvey having fun yet?

Knock-Knock.
  Who's there?
Hannah.
  Hannah who?
Hannah partridge in a pear tree.

Knock-Knock.
  Who's there?
Hammond.
  Hammond who?
Hammond eggs.

Knock-Knock.
  Who's there?
Iguana.
  Iguana who?
Iguana hold your hand.

Knock-Knock.
  Who's there?
Izzy.
  Izzy who?
Izzy come, Izzy go.

Knock-Knock.
  Who's there?
Isabella.
  Isabella who?
Isabella out of order?

Knock-Knock.
  Who's there?
Irish stew.
  Irish stew who?
**Irish stew would come
out and play.**

Knock-Knock.
Who's there?
Juno.
Juno who?
Juno what time it is?

Knock-Knock.
Who's there?
Justin.
Justin who?
Justin time for dinner.

Knock-Knock.
Who's there?
Jupiter.
Jupiter who?
Jupiter fly in my soup?

74

Knock-Knock.
Who's there?
Kenny.
Kenny who?
Kenny stay for dinner if he calls his mom?

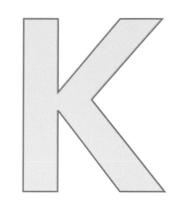

Knock-Knock.
Who's there?
Kareem.
Kareem who?
Kareem of wheat.

Knock-Knock.
Who's there?
Kimona.
Kimona who?
Kimona my house.

Knock-Knock.
Who's there?
Keith.
Keith who?
Keith me, you fool.

Knock-Knock.
Who's there?
Little old lady.
Little old lady who?
I didn't know you could yodel.

Knock-Knock.
Who's there?
Lion.
Lion who?
Lion here on your doorstep till you open the door.

76

Knock-Knock.
Who's there?
Lettuce.

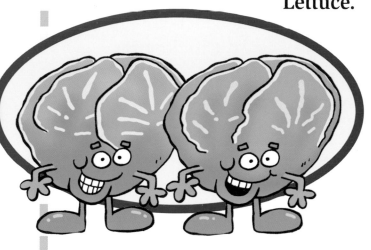

Lettuce who?
**Lettuce in and we'll
tell you another
knock-knock joke.**

Knock-Knock.
Who's there?
Luke.
Luke who?
Luke before you leap.

Knock-Knock.
Who's there?
Lois.
Lois who?
Lois man on the totem pole.

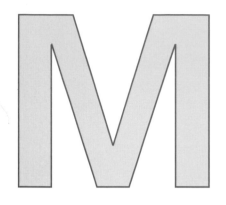

Knock-Knock.
 Who's there?
Megan, Elise, and Chicken.
 Megan, Elise, and Chicken who?
Megan, Elise — and Chicken it twice, gonna find out who's naughty and nice...

Knock-Knock.
 Who's there?
Mandy.
 Mandy who?
Mandy lifeboats — the ship's sinking!

Knock-Knock.
 Who's there?
Marmalade.
 Marmalade who?
"Marmalade an egg," said the little chicken.

Knock-Knock.
  Who's there?
Nona.
  Nona who?
Nona your business.

Knock-Knock.
  Who's there?
Needle.
  Needle who?
Needle little lunch.

Knock-Knock.
  Who's there?
Nadya.
  Nadya who?
Nadya head if you understand what I'm saying.

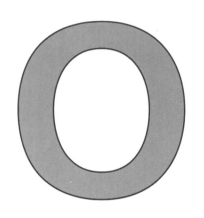

Knock-Knock.
   Who's there?
Oink oink.
   Oink oink who?
Are you a pig or an owl?

Knock-Knock.
   Who's there?
Omega.
   Omega who?
Omega up your mind.

Knock-Knock.
   Who's there?
Oscar and Greta.
   Oscar and Greta who?
Oscar foolish question, and Greta a foolish answer.

Knock-Knock.
    Who's there?
Police.
    Police who?
Police open the door.

Knock-Knock.
    Who's there?
Philippa.
    Philippa who?
Philippa bathtub, I'm dirty.

Knock-Knock.
    Who's there?
Pasta.
    Pasta who?
Pasta pizza.

Knock-Knock.
Who's there?
Quebec.
Quebec who?
**Quebec to the end
of the line.**

Knock-Knock.
Who's there?
Queen.
Queen who?
**Queen up your
room.**

Knock-Knock.
Who's there?
Quacker.
Quacker who?
**Quacker nother bad
joke and I'm leaving.**

Knock-Knock.
  Who's there?
Rocky.
  Rocky who?
Rocky-bye baby, on the treetop...

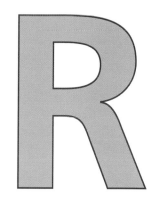

Knock-Knock.
  Who's there?
Rhoda.
  Rhoda who?
Rhoda boat.

Knock-Knock.
  Who's there?
Ringo.
  Ringo who?
Ringo round the collar.

Knock-Knock.
  Who's there?
Raven.
  Raven who?
Raven maniac.

S

Knock-Knock.
　Who's there?
Sancho.
　　Sancho who?
Sancho a letter but you never answered.

Knock-Knock.
　Who's there?
Siam.
　Siam who?
Siam your old pal.

Knock-Knock.
　Who's there?
Schick.
　Schick who?
Schick as a dog.

84

Knock-Knock.
Who's there?
Sarah.
Sarah who?
Sarah doctor in the house?

Knock-Knock.
Who's there?
Siamese.
Siamese who?
Siamese-y to please.

Knock-Knock.
Who's there?
Senior.
Senior who?
**Senior through the keyhole,
so I know you're in there.**

T

Knock-Knock.
  Who's there?
Theresa.
  Theresa who?
Theresa fly in my soup.

Knock-Knock.
  Who's there?
Toothache.
  Toothache who?
Toothache the high road and I'll take the low road....

Knock-Knock.
  Who's there?
Trigger.
  Trigger who?
Trigger treat!

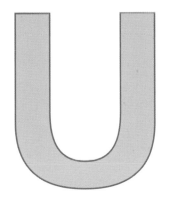

Knock-Knock.
Who's there?
Unaware.
Unaware who?
Unaware is what you put on first in the morning.

Knock-Knock.
Who's there?
Unity.
Unity who?
Unity sweater for me?

Knock-Knock.
Who's there?
Venice.
Venice who?
Venice lunch?

Knock-Knock.
Who's there?
Vanessa.
Vanessa who?
Vanessa you going to grow up?

Knock-Knock.
Who's there?
Vilma.
Vilma who?
Vilma frog turn into a prince?

Knock-Knock.
 Who's there?
Weasel.
 Weasel who?
Weasel while you work...

Knock-Knock.
 Who's there?
Weirdo.
 Weirdo who?
Weirdo you think you're going?

Knock-Knock.
 Who's there?
Wendy Katz.
 Wendy Katz who?
**Wendy Katz away,
the mice will play.**

Knock-Knock.
    Who's there?
Xavier breath.
    Xavier breath who?
Xavier breath — I'm not listening.

Knock-Knock.
    Who's there?
X.
    X who?
X for breakfast.

Knock-Knock.
    Who's there?
X.
    X who?
**X me no questions,
I'll tell you no lies.**

Knock-Knock.
   Who's there?
Yeti.
   Yeti who?
Yeti nother knock-knock joke.

Knock-Knock.
   Who's there?
Yah.
   Yah who?
Ride 'em, cowboy!

Knock-Knock.
　Who's there?
Zipper.
　Zipper who?
Zipper dee-doo-dah!

Knock-Knock.
　Who's there?
Zizi.
　Zizi who?
Zizi when you know how.

Knock-Knock.
　Who's there?
Zoe.
　Zoe who?
Zoe have come to the end of the chapter!

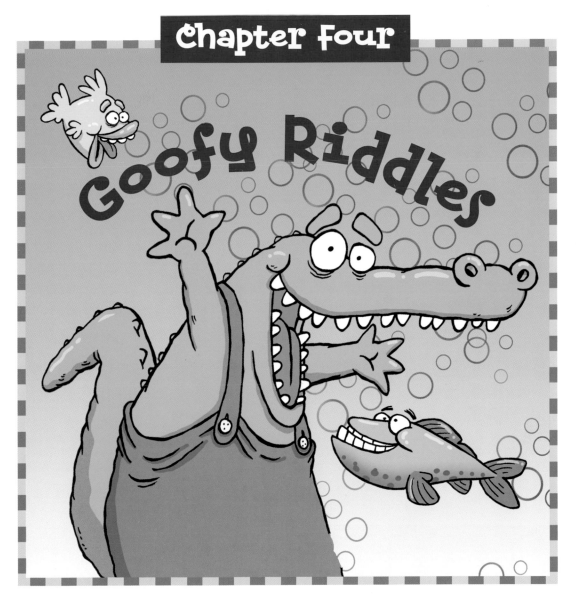

Chapter Four

Goofy Riddles

What would you get if you crossed a
kangaroo and a crocodile?
Leaping lizards!

How many balls of string would it take to reach the moon?
One, if it were long enough.

What do astronauts eat off?
Flying saucers.

What is an astronaut's favorite meal?
Launch.

How do you put a baby astronaut to sleep?
You rock-et.

What newspapers do
dinosaurs read?
   The Prehistoric Times.

How do you tell a dinosaur to hurry up?
   You say, "Shake a leg-o-saurus!"

Why did the dinosaur cross the road?
   Because in those days they didn't have chickens.

What prehistoric animal made noises in its sleep?
The dino-snore.

What would you get if a dinosaur stepped on your foot?
Ankylosaurus.

Where did prehistoric animals go for sun and fun?
To the dino-shore.

How long are a dinosaur's legs?
Long enough to reach the ground.

What would you get if you crossed a shark and a parrot?

An animal that talks your ear off.

What is quicker than a fish?
The one who catches it.

How do babies swim?
They do the crawl.

What do sea
monsters have
for lunch?
Fish and ships.

What does a shark eat
with peanut butter?
Jellyfish.

Where is the ocean deepest?
On the bottom.

What would you get if you crossed an
octopus and a cow?
An animal that could milk itself.

What would you get if you crossed an octopus and a cat?
**I don't know what you'd call it, but it would have
eight arms and nine lives.**

If you put three ducks in a carton, what would you get?
A box of quackers.

What did the chickens do in the health club?
Eggs-ercise.

What newspaper do cows read?
The Daily Moos.

Why shouldn't you tell a secret to a pig?
Because it is a squealer.

What insect can be spelled with just one letter?
Bee.

What do you call a young bee?
A babe-bee.

What would you get if you crossed an insect and a rabbit?
Bugs Bunny.

Why do bees hum?
Because they don't know the words.

What kind of gum do
bees chew?
Bumble gum.

What did the bee say to the flower?
"Hello, honey!"

What would you get if you crossed a dog and a waffle?
A woofle.

What do you have to
know before teaching
tricks to a dog?
More than the dog.

What do you call a dog
that graduates from
medical school?
Dog-tor.

How do dogs travel?
By mutt-a-cycle.

Why do dogs scratch themselves?
Because they are the only ones who know where it itches.

What is the best year
for a kangaroo?
Leap year.

Why did the kangaroo
mother scold her child?
**For eating crackers
in bed.**

Where does a kangaroo
go when it gets sick?
To the hop-ital.

Why do mother kangaroos hate rainy days?
Because then the children have to play inside.

What would you get if you crossed a laughing hyena with a cat?
A giggle puss.

Why is it dangerous to do math in the jungle?
Because if you add 4 and 4, you get 8.

Is it hard to spot a leopard?
No, they come that way.

What would you call a lion tamer who puts his right arm down a hungry lion's throat?
Lefty.

What do birds say on Halloween?
"Twick or tweet!"

What do ghosts have
with meatballs?
Spook-ghetti.

Why did Dracula go to the
orthodontist?
To improve his bite.

What do ghosts wear when it rains?
Ghoul-ashes.

What do witches eat at cookouts?
Halloweenies.

What is the first safety rule for witches?
Don't fly off the handle.

How can you tell twin witches apart?
It's not easy to tell which witch is which.

Why did the traffic light turn red?
So would you if you had to change in front of all those people.

If you crossed King Kong and a bell, what would you have?
A ding-dong King Kong.

What is brown, has a hump, and lives at the North Pole?
A lost camel.

What would you get if you crossed a chef and a rooster?
Cook-a-doodle-doo.

Why shouldn't you cry over spilled milk?
It gets too salty.

What is the best way to see flying saucers?
Scare the waitress.

What is a twip?

A twip is what a wabbit takes when he wides a twain.

What kind of geese are found in Portugal?

Portu-geese.

Where is Timbuktu?

Between Timbuk-one and Timbuk-three.

What did the little skunk want
to be when it grew up?
A big stinker.

What do people make that
you can't see?
Noise.

Why was the little lamb sent to
the principal's office?
Because it was baa-d.

What did one elevator say to the other elevator?
"I think I'm coming down with something."

What is black and white
and red all over?
A sunburned zebra.

What else is black and
white and red all over?
**A skunk with
diaper rash.**

What did the duck say when it fell in love with a parrot?
"Quacker wants a Polly."

Who does the ocean date?
It goes out with the tide.

What sound do two porcupines make when they kiss?
"Ouch!"

How many bricks does it take to finish a house?
Only one — the last one.

How can you tell that an elephant is in your refrigerator?
The door won't shut.

What did one garbage can say to the other?
Nothing. Garbage cans can't talk.

Where does a vampire take a bath?
In the bat-room.

What musical instrument is found in the bathroom?
A tuba toothpaste.

What is the best thing to eat in the bathtub?
Sponge cake.

What always speaks the truth but doesn't say a word?
A mirror.

What did the wig say to the head?
"I've got you covered."

What do frogs wear on
their feet in the summer?
Open toad shoes.

Where do cows go for entertainment?
To the moo-vies.

What is long, skinny, and beats
a drum?
Yankee Noodle.

Why couldn't Noah play cards on the ark?
**Because an elephant was standing on
the deck.**

What is the best way to talk
to the Frankenstein monster?
By long distance.

What animal talks a lot?
A yak.

What animal talks the
most?
A yakety yak.

Who always goes to
sleep with shoes on?
A horse.

What question can you never answer yes to?
"Are you asleep?"

What do baby sweet potatoes sleep in?
Their yammies.

What was Dr. Jekyll's favorite game?
Hyde and Seek.

What do dogs drink at parties?
Pupsi-cola.

What kind of bow can't be tied?
A rainbow.

How do you say
goodbye to a
mummy?
"BC'ing you!"